T0045281

Kitchen Science

Monica Halpern

Contents

Are You a Scientist?

Do you wonder about things? Are you curious? Scientists are. They ask questions. They look for possible answers.

Some scientists work in labs. Your kitchen can be your lab. You can use things that you find in your kitchen. You can be a kitchen scientist.

Observing

Scientists observe. That means they look at things closely. Observing helps scientists collect information. Observing helps scientists learn new things.

You observe with your eyes. Sometimes, you observe, or gather information, with your other senses, too. You observe by seeing, hearing, touching, smelling, or tasting.

Look closely at the man in the kitchen. Can you describe what he is doing? What items is he using?

When you describe exactly what you see,
you are observing like a scientist.

Measuring

Scientists measure. That means they find an exact amount. They use tools to measure to make their observations more exact. If someone describes something as "a little" or "a lot," you wouldn't know what the person means. But you know exactly what "one tablespoon" or "one hour" means.

Look at the three items on this page.

salt

flour

pizza

Which tool would you use to measure the different items?

timer

measuring cup

measuring spoons

When you use a tool to find an exact amount, you are measuring like a scientist.

Classifying

Scientists classify. That means they sort things into groups to show how they are alike. They might sort items by color, shape, size, or purpose. There are many different ways to classify.

Look at the items on these pages. Sort them into three groups. Which group would you put

- in the refrigerator?

- in the freezer?

- in the cabinet?

cereal

pasta

ice cream

frozen peas

juice

canned tomatoes

milk

red pepper

broccoli

When you sort things into groups,
you are classifying like a scientist.

Predicting

Scientists predict. That means they guess what will happen. They use what they know to make a good guess.

Look closely at the pictures on these pages. What do you observe? What do you predict will happen? Why?

When you use information you know to predict, you are acting like a scientist.

Experimenting

Scientists experiment. That means they test their predictions to see if they are right. They set up tests to see if their ideas are correct.

Look at the girl. She wants to get the catsup out of the bottle. She has an idea. She thinks adding air to the bottle will make the catsup flow faster. She tests her idea to see if it will work. Do you think her idea will work?

She puts a straw in the bottle and pushes it to the bottom. This puts air in the bottle.

After she takes out the straw, the catsup flows out of the bottle.

When you test an idea to see if it is right, you are acting like a scientist.

A Kitchen Experiment

Be a scientist in your kitchen. Try to answer this question:

What happens to raisins when they are soaked in water?

Make a prediction. Raisins are made by drying out grapes. Use what you know to make a good guess. Now, do an experiment to see if your prediction is right.

Here's What You Need:
- 20 raisins
- 2 plastic cups
- water

Here's What You Do:

1. Place 10 raisins in each cup.

2. Fill one cup with water.

3. Let the raisins stay covered with water for 6 to 8 hours.

4. Empty out the two cups. Compare the two groups of raisins.

Was your prediction right?

The raisins in the cup with water got bigger and rounder. When raisins are soaked in water, they go back to their original shape.

Be a Scientist

Observe   Use your senses to gather information.

Classify   Sort items that are alike into groups.

Measure   Use tools to find exact sizes or amounts.

Predict   Use what you know to tell what will happen. Make a good guess.

Experiment   Test to find out if a prediction is correct.